POEMS OF

Praise

AND

Pain

HEIDI KINNEY

www.heidikinney.com

CONTENTS

Introduction

While rummaging through a box filled with mementos from my childhood, I found a poem I wrote for a school assignment. Scrawled in red pen across the page is a note from my teacher: "Well done, as usual."

It's interesting to read the comment because it reminds me of my earlier self. I don't recall much from school, but I do remember that I took poetry seriously. I loved to read it, and I did my best to write it. In fact, I would write poems for anyone who showed an interest. Playing with words was one of my favorite pastimes. It still is!

Many times, words jump up and demand notice. They spin and frolic inside my head with such merriment and determination that I am compelled to write them down. Often, these words dance their way into a poem. Other times, they remain on scraps of paper, waiting patiently for me to remember why I wrote them in the first place.

Some poems in this collection began as scribbled words on bits of paper. This book features both recent and older poems. Some were written during the years described in my memoir, *Looking Back and Running Forward.*

Poetry speaks to each of us differently. That's one reason it's so special. We read and interpret it through our own unique perspective.

Sometimes poetry doesn't speak to us at all. We wonder what the poet was thinking. Why was the poem written? With each poem in this book, I included a personal message that offers something to ponder, a glimpse into my mind as I reflect on each poem. Read them or leave them. Whatever you decide, I pray you find a blessing in this book. I wrote it from my heart, a place of praise and pain, and I humbly hope it will touch yours.

It's not pleasant to talk about pain. It can make us feel uncomfortable. Often, we try to avoid it. We lock it away in an imaginary safe and pretend it doesn't exist.

But it does exist. Like it or not, pain is very real. It can knock us down in an instant. It can challenge us in ways that we've never known before.

Then there is praise. Praise lifts us up. It encourages us, and those around us, to keep going. Praise feels good.

Yet praise doesn't mean there's no pain. Can we earnestly express praise without also acknowledging pain? Does the former exist without the latter? Can you truly understand a smile without also knowing what it means to frown?

You will find both pain and praise in this book. There is sadness and joy. Acknowledge the one and you will more fully understand and appreciate the other. Having walked through the darkness, I can rejoice in the light.

Praise and Pain

Can there be good without the bad
Or day without the night?
Could we perceive the difference
Were both not in our sight?

How do we understand healing
Had the wound not come first?
Or be satisfied by water,
Without a touch of thirst?

And so it is with praise and pain.
Together, they are bound.
Rejoicing after the weeping,
A lost heart that's been found.

As babies learn to roll over, crawl, walk, or speak their first words, we are overjoyed. It's an amazing thing to witness! Each attempt at mastering a new skill is a cause for celebration. When they stumble and become frustrated, we encourage them to keep trying. When they do, we rejoice again.

As adults, we primarily focus on major achievements. We celebrate end results instead of the many steps it took to achieve them. However, just like babies, each step forward requires courage and persistence. You must have faith that your feet will land on solid ground, and you must rally the endurance to keep going even when it feels hard and when you falter.

It doesn't matter how far you go toward whatever goal you're chasing. Every step is significant and worthy of celebrating simply because you've chosen to take it.

Stepping Forward

Is there anything more beautiful
Than the simplicity
Of putting one foot
In front of the other
And moving forward
To a place that can only be better
Because you've taken the steps to get there?

There was a time when I felt powerless. I believed I had no control over my circumstances. Defeat could have been my middle name.

Thankfully, I did not remain in that state indefinitely. God revealed the lies I was believing and opened my eyes to see a way forward.

We can't control the difficulties we face in life any more than we can control the dark clouds in the sky. However, what we can control is how we respond to them when they come. We can either waste our precious time focusing on the negative, or we can concentrate on the positive because we know the trials of life will make us stronger.

Dark Cloud

I defy you, dark cloud.
You cannot defeat me.
I shall not waste a moment
Staring at your threatening form.
You will not control my happiness today.
Though you linger,
And almost beckon me to be weary,
I shall not succumb.
I will rejoice in this day
Even if you spread to cover the vast sky
With your gloominess.
Hold fast your raindrops
Because they will be of no use.
Their dampness will not penetrate me.
If your showers fall,
I will see them as a cleansing of my soul,
Preparing me for growth.
So, I reject you, dark cloud,
For my sunshine resides within.

When my husband died, I struggled as a single mother. At the time, our youngest son was an infant, and his brother was two years old. It was a challenge just to make it to the end of each day without collapsing from mental and physical exhaustion.

On many evenings, my reward for successfully getting through another day was a glass of wine. Maybe that doesn't sound like a poor choice. One glass of wine is fine, isn't it? It may be for some, but it wasn't for me. I came to believe that I needed that wine. What I really needed was to rest.

Even when we have the very best of intentions, we can stumble. We listen to the lies of the world and ignore what's in our hearts. One seemingly miniscule step toward a shady path can lead us astray. Before we know it, we are pulled so far in the wrong direction that we give up, convinced that all is lost.

Pay attention to the little decisions you make each day and the voices you act on. It's never too late to choose another path.

The Serpent

Slow and steady creeps the serpent.
As a predator stalking its prey,
It slithers in and begins to entangle.
Its victim too detached to sense its touch.
Speaking lies as it coils
Round and round.
So heavy with its weight,
The hunted collapses.
The burden is too great.
Rejoicing in his craftiness,
The serpent retreats,
Adding another sinner
To his trophy case.

Sometimes people talk about the stages of grief as if they are items on a list to be checked off. Finished with stage one? Check. Move on to stage two.

This type of thinking implies that there is an ending, a final box to be checked. Complete that step and grief is finished. Unfortunately, it doesn't really work that way.

Grief comes in waves, and with those waves comes sadness. Some days that sadness is intense and other days it's mild. Sometimes, you can barely feel the sadness at all.

"When the Sadness Comes" was written during a time when I experienced more intense days than mild. If you've never felt this way, consider yourself fortunate. If you have, I'm deeply sorry. May you experience many joyful days ahead.

When the Sadness Comes

When the sadness comes,
I go numb to my surroundings.
I feel no pleasure and no pain, only cold.
My eyes stare blankly into nothingness.
I can't even bring myself to cry,
When the sadness comes.

When the sadness comes,
I lose track of the hours as daytime turns to night.
Mealtimes are forgotten
And tasks go undone.
All common sense leaves my being
When the sadness comes.

When the sadness comes,
It draws every ounce of strength,
Sucking me dry until I am a heap on the floor.
And there I stay, unable to move,
Without the slightest idea of how I got there,
Or why I would want to leave,
When the sadness comes.

Trust is hard. Admitting that we're afraid is also difficult. Sometimes life feels easier to bear when we attempt to control everything. If we can control all aspects of our lives, then we don't have to trust, or so we like to tell ourselves. But this is an impossible task since we can't possibly control everything. Even if we could, why do we assume that our way would be best?

Patience is also hard. We don't like to wait for things. So, instead of waiting, we act. We do our own thing and forget about all else, even when it means we'll sacrifice what we really desire. To our impatient selves, action is better than waiting.

I wrote "Trust" many years ago, and I have grown in my faith since then. However, sometimes I still struggle with trust. I suspect it's a lesson I'll have to keep on learning.

Trust

Here I am again
Wrestling with uncertainty.
Why don't I trust you enough
To release the fear?
I plot.
I scheme.
I attempt to forge my own way.
If you won't show me a path,
I'll make my own
Knowing full well
It may lead to hardship.
How easily, I convince myself.
Have I learned nothing?

I'm continually amazed at the beauty and complexity of God's creation. I marvel at how the birds know exactly what they're supposed to do. It's easy to envy them. Sometimes we can become so consumed with worrying about fulfilling an extraordinary worthwhile objective that we forget to focus on the moment we're in.

There have been many times in my life when I questioned my worth. Sometimes these coincided with listening to a sermon about gifts and talents. It always sounded simple: Use your gifts and talents and you'll find your calling. The problem was, I didn't think I had any gifts or talents. What was my purpose? I agonized over this question repeatedly.

Over time, I came to realize that I didn't need to worry. All I really needed to do was to serve the Lord every day in whatever way I'm able. What I do each day may not be remarkable in the eyes of the world, but I'm not living for the eyes of man. I'm living for the one who created this beautiful world surrounding me.

Birds and Trees

With every shade of green before my eyes,
I stare and wonder at the majesty and diversity
Of your creation.
Each one existing with its own uniqueness and design,
Yet coexisting in harmony.
All part of a perfect plan.
A robin hunts for treasures in the soil
And pulls a worm nearly as long as its body into its beak
And continues its quest.
It doesn't stop to question its purpose.
It doesn't ask for directions.
Like the trees, it just seeks its nourishment
From the Earth you created
And fulfills the tasks
You have programmed it to do.
Oh, that I should be more
Like the birds and the trees.

How do you greet each day? Do you wake to an alarm and react with moaning and groaning? Or, do you rejoice because you're looking forward to whatever the day may bring? Or maybe you're like me, and do a little of both depending on the day.

I wrote "A Single Choice" and "Glorious Morning" on two very different days. I wish I could say that most mornings I gravitate more toward the feelings in "Glorious Morning," but that wouldn't be true.

When your back is aching or you're especially tired because you didn't sleep well, it's difficult to be cheerful. It's easier to let your body dictate your mood for the day.

However, even worse than spending the day cranky is getting to the end of the day and realizing that it could have been better if you had only made a different choice in attitude that morning. A simple choice can have an enormous impact.

A Single Choice

I chose defeat today,
A bitter slimy pill.
I swallowed it quickly.
Its effects lasted all day.
Colors dulled to gray.
Sounds morphed to humming.
A day wasted by a single choice.

Glorious Morning

Oh, glorious morn, you come again!
What treasures do you have in store?
What tasks do you have for me today?
I am renewed and ready to begin,
And thankful for another day to serve.

Life is full of decisions. With each decision comes the possibility of a positive or negative result. Unfortunately, it's impossible to know ahead of time which one we'll get. We use our knowledge and experience to guide us, but every choice involves some risk.

Sometimes the fear of making a wrong choice is so great that we refuse to choose at all. We become passive and let others make decisions for us. Or we remain frozen in our indecision until the circumstances of life force us to move.

For a long time, I agonized over the decision to sell our rental property. I wanted the burden of it gone, but I couldn't bring myself to sell it. The fear of making a poor financial decision overwhelmed me. In the end, I could have saved our family countless stressful situations if I had made the choice sooner.

Making decisions, especially important ones, can be difficult, but we will never get to where we need to go by refusing to make them.

Indecision

Here I hover in the middle,
Smack dab between starting over
And giving up.
Doing just enough to stay suspended.
Afraid to move.
Afraid to rest.
Held captive with invisible irons.
Release me, Lord, of these entanglements.
Let me move forward
On your path.
Don't leave me here in my indecision.

For years, I struggled with anxiety and depression. There is a common misconception that someone diagnosed with depression feels down every day. That's not been my experience. Some days were good, and some were bad. At first, there were more bad days than good. Later, there were more good days than bad.

I originally wrote "Some Days Up, Some Days Down" as an entry for a poetry competition that aimed to highlight the role of creativity in mental health. Although I didn't win a prize, I felt honored knowing my poem was displayed with the other entries during the exhibition in London. It was my hope then that it spoke to someone there and brought a sense of normality and encouragement, and it is my hope now that it does the same as it's presented here.

Some Days Up, Some Days Down

Some days up.
Some days down.
Still, the world goes round and round.
Am I here? Yes, half the time
When my life is all in line.
Some days up.
Some days down.
Label not my ailing mind.
I'll pass your tests.
I'm doing fine.
Some days up.
Some days down.
How many days are wasted then
While I'm nestled in my den
Pretending life's come to an end?
Some days up.
Some days down.
Today, the sun shines new and bright
And I'm lifted by its light,
Strengthened to keep up the fight.
Some days up.
Some days down.
And my pen is ever near,
Capturing thoughts when they are clear,
Sucking the breath out of my fear.
Some days up.
Some days down.

Have people ever told you they made a decision based on something you said, or did something because you did it first? You might not even remember saying or doing what they're talking about.

Our words and actions have consequences. They are important. Friends, family, and even strangers may look to us for inspiration when we don't even know they're looking. A seemingly meaningless comment, in person or online, could bring someone a smile or a tear, encouragement or defeat.

You may feel your words and actions don't matter, but everything you do sends a message. Whether you realize it or not, you are impacting someone, or several others, by your choices. Unbeknownst to you, someone may be searching for hope, courage, or meaning. Will you show them the sunshine or lead them into the darkness?

Show Me Your Sunshine

Show me your sunshine.
For I linger in darkness
With no glimpse of the light.
Show me what moves you
Beyond a rut of complacency
Into a day filled with purpose
That I may glean from your experience
And reach toward the source
That feeds your soul.

Have you ever stopped to think about how many things we break on purpose? We tear through the skin of an orange to get to the sweet fruit beneath it, or we crush herbs to release their aroma and flavor. It's only through an act of perceived destruction that the hidden potential is realized.

The same is true about us. With every obstacle or hardship, we break in some way. Although we wouldn't deliberately choose adversity, that doesn't mean it isn't valuable. It can unlock something in us that we didn't even know was there.

Broken

As a peppercorn is ground,
Or an almond is cracked,
As a watermelon is sliced,
Or a grape is smashed,
So, too, am I broken,
Carefully and deliberately,
For a greater purpose.

Living your life without a significant other is hard. Some days, like the one described in "Alone in the Pew," are more challenging than others. Sometimes the loneliness creeps in when you aren't expecting it.

Even when you're accustomed to going places alone, it's not always easy. It takes courage to force yourself into a situation where you might stand out. Staying home is easier. Staying home can distract you from your loneliness.

If you're the one alone in the pew, or somewhere else, take heart. Your bravery is commendable. Even the roughest days can't steal that away from you.

Alone in the Pew

Alone in the pew.
How did I get here and why does it bother me today?
The emptiness on either side taunts me.
Lord, are you here?
I am all alone.
Please come sit with me.
For a second, I imagine you are next to me,
But only for a second.
I console myself with the thought you are always with me.
Why don't I feel better?

Being a Christian doesn't mean your life is flawless, that you won't make mistakes. It also doesn't mean you won't suffer. Life is hard for everyone.

Even so, the world promotes the illusion of perfection. Because of this, we sometimes torture ourselves with unrealistic expectations. When we don't live up to the impossible standard, we feel miserable.

When we're struggling, we may try to pretend that everything is fine. We paint a picture of ourselves that's untrue and mask our tears so no one will see our pain. We put on a show.

Unfortunately, hiding our hurt helps no one. We are being dishonest with ourselves and everyone else when we pretend. It's far easier to relate to someone who shares their pain than someone who pretends to be perfect.

We don't have to pretend. There's someone who knows all our imperfections and loves us anyway. I'm thankful for that!

So, I Pretend

I know your joy should fill me,
That I should shine from deep within,
But sadness overflows my soul
Until I'm drowning with my sin.

So, I pretend.

What mockery kept locked away.
What deep regret held tight inside.
Tormented, torn, masked, tearful eyes,
But you know all I hide.

Still, I pretend.

A witness? Oh, Lord, I am a poor one.
Hidden away from the world in fear.
What gifts have I to offer anyway,
Except a broken heart and surplus tears?

So, I pretend.

I overdo. I overthink.
Completely consumed by over trying.
Soon all I can do is sit and stare
Ignoring the world as if it's dying.

Until I can pretend.

And I'm not a good pretender.
You can see it in my eyes.
My face is dim, my body limp,
It cannot tell the lie.

I guess I can't pretend.

Why, Lord, do I feel empty?
I long to do your will.
Please cleanse me of this darkness
And let my mind be still.

Sometimes when we sing hymns at church, I get lost in the words. With their meter and rhyme, they could reside in a book of poetry. I'd like to sit for a while, ponder them, and admire their beauty.

Although I'm not a songwriter, once in a while, a poem comes to my mind as a song. It's odd because as I'm writing the words, I can almost hear the tune playing in my head. Perhaps it's just a melody I've heard before that my brain is putting words to.

"Singing with the Lord" is a poem that came to me as a song. Maybe you will hear the melody too.

Singing with the Lord

Lord, I'm tired,
So very tired,
And I barely have the strength inside to stand.
Yes, I'm tired.
My bones are tired.
Will you help to hold me up so I don't fall?

> Rest in me.
> Abide in me.
> Lay your head upon my shoulder for relief.
> Look to me.
> I am here.
> I have brought you to the place you need to be.

Lord, I'm weary.
My soul is dreary,
And I question and I tremble with my fear.
Oh, how I've fallen.
I feel forgotten.
Will you leave me here to wallow in my grief?

> Come to me.
> I'm not far.
> Seek me through my word and you will see.
> I've not gone.
> I'm close at hand.
> I could lift you up if you would just believe.

How long, Lord, must I wait here?
I've been here for so long.
The years fly past without me.
I'm stuck within my bond.
The seasons change, my children grow,
And I am still alone.
I've loved and lost. My heart is dry.
Will you punish me until I die?

> Come back to me.
> I'm still here.
> You've forgotten all your blessings, how I care.
> Pray to me.
> Spend time with me.
> I have plans for you that I would like to share.

Forgive me, Lord.
I come to you.
I am broken, and I long to see your face.
My heart is yours,
And all I am.
Thank you for your unrelenting grace.

Do you write New Year's resolutions? Often, when we write resolutions or goals, we concentrate on tangible things. Maybe we want to exercise every day, or finish a project, or travel to a new destination. Once we achieve our goal, we move on to the next item on the list. Sometimes we even celebrate our achievement.

The poem "Small Victories" is a resolution list of a different sort. It speaks to the small choices we make every day and why they are worth celebrating.

You don't need to wait until the beginning of a new year for a new beginning. Every new day is a new opportunity. Focus on what matters most and rejoice each time you do.

Small Victories

This year I will celebrate
Small victories.
When I choose to
Give instead of take,
Listen instead of speak,
Move instead of sit,
Breathe instead of scream,
Or trust instead of worry,
I will celebrate.
Though small are the victories,
They are victories just the same.
Each time that I choose
To act on the light
Instead of the darkness,
I grow closer
To the person I long to be.
And that is worth celebrating.

If you're a parent, you probably know how it feels to make sacrifices. Children have needs. As parents, our job is to provide for those needs even at the expense of our own.

Sometimes, like when you're tired at the end of the day, this feels especially difficult. We can feel overwhelmed by our role. We can lose sight of what's important.

I wrote "Nighttime" many years ago. It's a moment in time, a snapshot of my life back then, when I felt challenged every day as a single mother of two young boys. It was a struggle, and I didn't always have the best attitude. I'm thankful that on this night, I chose to view the situation through the lens of peace.

Nighttime

A light head upon my shoulder sleeps,
Complete surrender at my side.
The slightest movement and he stirs.
Is this peace or is it prison?
I cannot move.
I try to appreciate the time.
After all, it will not always be like this.
Not that any moment is ever like the next,
At least not in its entirety.
So, I resolve myself that this is peace.
A frightened toddler seeking comfort in the night
From a mother who loves him.
What could be more peaceful than that?

Loss comes in many forms. We suffer loss when we lose a loved one. Loss also comes when we experience changes in our health, relationships, finances, and lifestyles.

No matter the source of the loss, we sometimes torture ourselves by thinking about what could have been if the loss had not happened. We paint a picture in our minds of an imagined future and mourn that loss as well.

However, the picture in our minds is only an illusion. It's impossible for us to accurately predict our futures based on past experiences and events. Every moment touches the next and sets a new path.

It's madness to mourn an imagined loss. Surely, one loss is more than enough.

Madness

How mad to grieve what could have been!
How ludicrous the notion!
Built on an impossible premise
That somehow an imagined future
Could stem from an unaltered past
In an ever-changing world of motion.

I wrote "Tomorrow" in late 2020 when the world was filled with uncertainty from the pandemic. However, the poem speaks to any tough season when we feel lost and stuck.

Just because you can't see the light at the end of the tunnel, that doesn't mean it isn't there. It might just mean that you're not ready to see it. Sometimes you must wait where you are until it's the right time to move forward. You may be discouraged, but don't give up. A new dawn is coming.

Tomorrow

Tomorrow there will be sunshine,
And smiles,
And friends.
But I can't see that now.
Tomorrow there will be laughter,
And singing,
And praise.
But I can't hear that now.
Tomorrow there will be handshakes,
And hugs,
And happiness
But I can't feel that now.
Today there is darkness,
And silence,
And loneliness.
They penetrate my soul
And seek to destroy me.
Yet even though I cannot see,
Nor hear,
Nor feel
The goodness of tomorrow,
A glowing ember remains in my heart
Placed lovingly there to remind me
A new dawn is coming.

In a world ruled by differing opinions and beliefs, it can be difficult to demonstrate one's faith without being judged, criticized, or labeled. People poke fun at things they don't understand, or at things that make them feel uncomfortable.

Sometimes people would rather label someone else than take a hard look at themselves. It's not easy to admit that you're a sinner in need of a savior. It's easier to call Christians crazy than admit that you wished you had their faith.

There was a time when I had no faith. I didn't know what Christians believed, or why they behaved the way they did. Thankfully, God opened my eyes. I'm a different person than I was before, and I'm grateful for that.

Crazy Christian

Assign your label
If you must.
I'll still speak the truth
In which I trust.

I'll hold no vengeance
Against the sin.
You know not what
You're living in.

Until you're broken,
Led to your knees,
You cannot grasp
The world I see.

So, call me crazy
If it helps you deal.
I'll hold on tightly
To a love that's real.

We can be our own worst enemy, especially when we're tired. It's then that our defenses go down and we're more likely to believe false truths about ourselves.

For me, just before dinner is usually a difficult time. I'm tired, hungry, and feel pressured to get food prepared for my family. Of course, the pressure is all in my head. I have a preconceived idea, a glorified fantasy, of what dinner time should look like. When I fail to live up to my unrealistic expectations, as I always do, I become irritable and doubt my worth.

Ignoring the lies that sneak into our minds is challenging, but becoming more aware of their presence can help. They don't need to defeat you. You can always fight back with the truth.

Like a Lion

Like a lion stalking its prey
You lie in wait 'till the moment's right.
Mid-afternoon or early evening
Are your favorite times to pounce,
When the weariness has set in.
My body aches,
And I'm oblivious to the impending attack.
You sink your teeth deep.
Yet I'm so worn that I don't feel the pain.
You tear me into pieces with your lies
Until I bleed out defeat
By forgetting my truth.
Oh, that I could learn to resist
The schemes of my tired mind.

When was the last time you gazed in awe at the beauty of the morning sun as it paints the world with light?

We often rush through our days and fail to appreciate our surroundings. We let the day unfold without ever really embracing it. Instead of taking notice of the people and wonders around us, we spend spare moments on mindless tasks.

"Wake Me Up" is a prayer, a plea to God for help in stopping this behavior. Life is overflowing with blessings, but we won't experience them if we're too busy.

Wake Me Up

When I fail to notice the morning sun,
Or hear the blissful tune of singing birds,
Shake me out of my stupor.
When I sleepwalk through the day
And forget to smile,
Wake me up.
Darkness lies in the cracks,
Stealing priceless moments from oblivious prey.
Open my eyes, Lord, that I may continually see
The beauty, the blessings, surrounding me.

It's curious how you can see an object and instantly identify with it. Even something small and seemingly unremarkable, like a pebble, can speak to how you're feeling on a particular day.

In keeping with the size of a pebble, this poem is short. Sometimes, a few words are all you need.

Pebble

Today I am a pebble on a barren ground.
Hard.
Cold.
Jagged.
Motionless.
Displaced.
Waiting to be tread upon.

Pebbles take on a new meaning in the poem "Strength." Here they are nothing more than a minor nuisance compared to rocks that felt like boulders.

Everyone has a load to carry. You have responsibilities and stressors that you alone must bear. You may have painful experiences in your past, or you may be walking through a difficult time right now.

Some days will feel harder than others, but your perception will likely change over time. You can choose to be thankful for that.

Strength

Some days the burden is heavy.
My body trembles and my heart aches from the load.
Still, it's mine to carry.
As unbearable as it is today,
Tomorrow it may seem lighter.
The rocks that felt like boulders years ago
Would feel like pebbles now, like trivial inconveniences.
And though I would not have chosen
The load that I have carried,
It has strengthened me beyond measure.
It has made me who I am today
And will make me who I am tomorrow.

"Comfy in the Corner" is for anyone who's ever been afraid to take a risk. It could be something as simple as trying an unfamiliar food, going somewhere new, speaking up for yourself, or choosing to do something in a different way than you've ever done it before.

Moving out of your comfort zone can be hard. We like to stick with what we know because it makes us feel safe. To ease our anxiety, we convince ourselves that our way is the best way and choose the same way every time.

Sometimes, though, we get left behind when we refuse to make a change. We deny ourselves the opportunity to learn and grow from new experiences.

It may be easier to stick with what's familiar, but you'll never know what you're missing until you step out of the corner.

Comfy in the Corner

Comfy in the corner.
Securely seated in my place.
I don't know how I got here,
But this is where I'll stay.

Comfy in the corner.
I have everything I need.
I'm alone, and I'm forgotten,
But the quiet is serene.

Comfy in the corner.
I'm not hiding. I'm not scared.
It's better to be safe here
Than risk life over there.

Comfy in the corner.
Dying slowly day by day.
I wonder what it'd be like
If I didn't want to stay.

It's not difficult to get pulled into a negative mindset when you fill your brain with one-sided doom and gloom messages. You absorb what you hear and then unknowingly distribute this negativity to those around you with your words and actions.

Writing poetry helps clear my head. I wrote "Politics" when I was extremely frustrated and disappointed with the negative messages being spread that contradicted scripture.

Sometimes you need to step back and question what you're listening to. Does it line up with what you claim to believe as truth? Or, are you allowing yourself to be misled by someone else's agenda?

Politics

Don't preach to me your politics
For I'm loyal to my king.
He chooses whom he uses.
He's at work in everything.
Enough with all the chatter
Of conspiracies and schemes.
It sounds like you've forgotten
What a trusting servant means.
Don't be deceived by discontentment.
The darkness there is strong.
Let go, then step forward
Into the light where you belong.

It's not easy being the primary caretaker for a loved one who is battling a life-threatening illness. You are on call all the time. You set aside all else to do whatever you can to provide the best care, often at the expense of your own well-being.

Breaks are hard to come by, but when they do come, you are so stressed from your responsibilities that your mind can't relax. Sometimes breaks are not breaks at all, but time to do a task for your loved one. It doesn't matter though, because time is extremely precious when you're a caregiver. A moment away is a moment lost.

What happens to a caregiver when the person being cared for dies? That is the focus of "Bereaved." The poem describes a moment I experienced several weeks after the death of my husband. I remember it vividly. It was the first time I mentally acknowledged my caregiver role was over.

Bereaved

It's an odd sort of feeling
When the world stops spinning,
And you're left just sitting
And catching your breath.
What a peculiar sensation,
To no longer be needed,
'Cause the weight's been lifted
Though you prayed it would stay.
Caught in a juxtaposition
Between guilt and submission.
Your body betrays you
As it renders a sigh.
A table of strangers
Filled with judgement and anger,
But your mind can't see them.
You're too empty inside.

Have you ever had the wind knocked out of you? It's a terrible feeling. You're completely helpless until you regain your breath.

Sometimes the pain you experience while grieving is a similar sensation, except it can be more intense, like what I describe in the poem "Grief."

The pain of grief can come out of nowhere and suddenly slam you to the ground. All you can do is attempt to breathe and wait for it to pass.

Grief

When the pain arrives,
I lose my breath.
My heart stops beating
For a moment.
My mind freezes in a flash
As I stare aimlessly.
So quickly it comes
Without warning,
An invisible train bounding into a station
Without the slightest sound.
There is no time to prepare,
And no way to prevent its arrival.
To attempt an escape is futile
Because it will find you,
And always when you least expect it.
It tears, burns, and clenches at my being
Until I sink into myself,
Until it is gone,
Hiding in wait
For another day.

There was a time when I believed someone else had the answer to whatever problem I thought I had. I just needed to read the right book to fix my issue. Bedtime was the time I used to pour into my brain as much information as possible. It became a problem.

Don't get me wrong, I'm a firm believer in research and learning, but sometimes we go searching for answers we already have. I don't know if we forget we have the answers, or if we just don't trust ourselves enough to act on them. Or maybe we don't like the answers we have, so we go looking for someone to tell us something different. Whatever the case, sometimes we just need to trust what we know, close the book, and go to sleep.

Bedtime

Searching, always searching,
A pile of books to be finished.
Longing, endless longing,
The answer is there somewhere.
Tiring, achingly tiring,
I just need to keep reading.
Resisting, defiantly resisting,
My eyes and brain conspire against me.
Submitting, begrudgingly submitting,
Mark my place for tomorrow.

I'm not sure if anyone has actually ever told me I'm stubborn, but I know I am. This stubbornness shows itself in many different ways. One way is by trying to keep my emotions hidden when I feel like I'm falling apart.

"Obstinate" is a poem that expresses this stubborn attitude, but also reveals the struggle behind it. Sometimes we try to hide our pain, but God knows we're hurting. We can cry out to Him for help.

Obstinate

I'm close to tears but I won't cry
Gotta hold my head up high.
I feel the pain, but I won't bleed.
Can't let them see my need.
I'm close to tears, but I can't cry.
Gotta keep these brown eyes dry.
The ache inside my heart is fierce.
Clear thoughts inside my mind are scarce.
But you know it all. You put me here.
You know my pain, my strife, my fear.
I try to stand with a grateful heart
But bit by bit, I fall apart.
Cleanse me, Lord, and make me whole.
Lift the burden of this toll.
Anguish, hurt, and misery
How can this be your plan for me?

Are you a half-empty or half-full kind of person? An optimist or pessimist? Maybe you're optimistic about some things and pessimistic about other things.

Whether you feel more inclined to positivity or negativity, one thing I've learned is that you get to decide which to act on. You have a choice. Your behavior and attitude are under your control.

I'm not saying it's always easy to look on the bright side. When external pressures are weighing you down, it can be extremely difficult. I've let stress get the best of me countless times and made poor choices as a result.

Sometimes we just need to pause in the moment and remind ourselves of who we are and who we want to be. Then, with a calm and rational state of mind, we can choose where to cast our gaze.

It's Your Choice

Where will you cast your gaze today?
Will you look to the sky
Or look to the ground?
Will you reach your arms high,
Breathe deep,
And fill yourself with life?
Or, will you lower your eyes
And stumble in the darkness?
The choice is yours.
Where will you cast your gaze today?

Have you ever stopped to think about how many things you do each day without really thinking about them? You reach for a light switch and your arm unconsciously knows exactly how high to lift, and your fingers know precisely where to go. Or you get up in the night in darkness and can move around your home with ease. Or you instinctively clasp the hand of a loved one.

It's amazing how quickly and easily the body adjusts to changes and learns new movement patterns, like when you rearrange furniture. It doesn't take long at all to forget how things used to be. Yet, the body responds differently with the loss of a loved one. At least, that's been my experience.

My late husband and I were hand holders. I wrote "Instinct" one day when I noticed that my right arm was outstretched as if it was searching for his hand to hold even though it wasn't there, and it hadn't been there in a very long time.

Instinct

In the quiet of the night
My heart still searches for you.
Though my mind wanders to and fro
With the happenings of the day,
My hand still reaches for yours
Only to find,
Time and again,
That it's not there.
Will my body ever forget?
Forget the comfort of your embrace,
Or the warmth of your touch?

Have you ever experienced a season when everything felt difficult? This was me when my children were little. At times, I would try to write my feelings to clear my head. On the day I wrote this poem, what came to me were simple adjectives.

It's difficult for me to read this poem now. I wish I could go back and give my younger self a hug and tell her that everything would be alright, but that's not possible. Even if it was, I may not have believed it then. I wasn't ready.

Sometimes you just have to walk through whatever difficulty you're facing, one small step at a time. It may feel like the season will never end, but it will. Identifying how you're feeling may help you cope, even if that means just writing a few adjectives on a blank page.

Adjectives of the Day

Cluttered
Surrounded by baskets of tasks to be done

Cramped
Pushed to the edge of my bed by a sleeping child

Drained
Exhausted of all logical thought and potential for joy

Overwhelmed
Bombarded with decisions to be made...alone

Isolated
Locked inside my little messy world

Frightened
Taunted by the feeling that I am not living as I should

As you enter our home, one of the first things you see is a charming antique dresser. It has beautiful ornate features and a lovely, stained finish. However, it wasn't always this way.

When my late husband bought this piece of furniture at a yard sale many years ago, I thought he was bonkers. At the time, it was fully covered with old grimy pink and white paint. I didn't understand why he wanted it.

However, I wasn't looking at it the same way he was. He saw beyond the layers of gunk and knew that buried beneath the paint was gorgeous wood waiting to be uncovered.

Sometimes we can get buried by the burdens of life. We can lose sight of ourselves and almost forget who we are. Perhaps if we do some refinishing, we will uncover the beauty beneath our own surface.

Cobwebs

In the cobwebbed corner of my brain,
There lies an ancient memory
Of a girl who dreamed, sang, and wrote.
And achieved many things.
I can't see her,
But I sense that she's here
Somewhere buried
Beneath the dust of torment and trouble.

Our society has many phrases to console someone who is grieving. One thing people say is that the deceased person will always be with you in your heart. Sometimes, though, the person is hiding elsewhere.

My kids and I regularly played a version of the game hide-and-seek when they were young. Occasionally, I still try to play it with my two dogs even though I'm not sure they truly understand the point of the game.

"Hide and Seek" is a playful and honest account of some places I've found my late husband. I never know when and where I'll find him.

Hide and Seek

I found you today quite unexpectantly
Hiding in the lyrics of a song.
How cleverly you camouflaged
Until the chorus came along.
And yesterday you were in the basement
With the boxes and the tools,
And the piles of unknown items,
The things I'll never use.
Last week, you sought to tease me,
When you were deceptively disguised,
With just a portion reappearing
In the gaze of our son's eyes.
How odd this game of hide and seek.
I don't even try to play.
Yet I always seem to find you
Even though you've gone away.

Several years ago, I began running on a regular basis. I didn't know back then how much it would help me grow physically and mentally, nor did I know how much it would correlate to my spiritual journey.

Sometimes you give of yourself all you believe you have to give. You don't think you can take another step. You're ready to quit because you've already preset a limit on your capabilities.

It's been my experience, in running and in life, that when you reach your perceived end, the Lord is always there for you. He supports you and leads you on to something more, something you didn't think was possible. All you need to do is trust Him.

The Journey

I run until
I come to the end of myself,
My body drained.
It is there that the Lord shows me
Another step,
A step I couldn't see before,
And never knew was there waiting.
He renews my strength
And leads me on.
Joyous cries fill the air.
Or perhaps they're in my mind.
As I am overwhelmed by the blessing
Of a never-ending journey.

Sometimes we surround ourselves with so much commotion we become overstimulated. We may not even realize how much the world is affecting us until we begin to feel lost.

The wonderful news is you aren't actually lost. You are still you, and you can always find yourself again, in solitude.

There's something powerful that happens when you spend quiet time alone. It's a small thing, but it can have a huge positive impact on your quality of life.

In Solitude

In solitude,
I find myself.
Breathing deep, the tension fades
As I remember who I am.
Thankful for the reunion,
And the reminder,
That I can always find the way back
To myself
In solitude.

Some say that people never change. I disagree. Although I still hold many character traits and interests that I've held for years, I'm not the same person I used to be. I've transformed over time.

Sometimes I wonder whether my late husband would even recognize me today. What would he think of this new version of me? "Would You Love Me" explores this idea.

Would You Love Me

Would you love me
As I am today
If we could have the chance to meet?
A woman hardened,
Yet stronger for it.
Would you still fancy
This shadow of my former self?
With my tired eyes
And sagging skin.
Still playing in the garden
And admiring the freedom of the birds.
Still singing when no one is listening
And sitting by an open window with a notebook.
A woman wise from years of solitude.
Bolder, fiercer, braver, kinder.
Would you love the woman I've become?
It matters not, I suppose,
Since this version of me
Only exists
In a world without you.

Above a doorway in our home is the phrase "count your blessings." It reminds me I have much to be thankful for.

All too often, we forget how much we're blessed. We focus on the negative and cast a shadow over our lives and the lives of those around us.

"Sing Praises" is a reminder that we have power over the darkness. When we adopt an attitude of gratitude and sing praises despite our circumstances, we become shining beacons of light.

Sing Praises

Sing praises with a thankful heart.
Fixate not on fear.
Words of glory are never wasted.
They are sparks that ignite a fire
And bring light to the darkness.

Years ago, I watched a fascinating documentary about the use of music as a therapy for patients with memory loss. When the music played, patients that had appeared miserable and almost lifeless before unexpectedly transformed into another version of themselves. They became happy and animated. It was like the music had flipped a switch on in their brains.

Music is powerful. It can bring us back in an instant to another time and place. Suddenly, we can recall little details with amazing clarity.

When we listen to music, we sometimes step back into our former self and relive emotions. These may be happy feelings, or they may be painful. Sometimes there may be a little of both.

Sanctuary

Oh, blessed tune,
You take me back
To a midnight hour,
A crying baby,
And an exhausted young mother.
What power you have
To stir my soul,
To bring sadness and joy,
And memories long forgotten,
Yet still lingering
In the dormant chambers of my mind,
Waiting patiently to be resurrected
To remind me of the journey.

Do you ever fall prey to the negative voices in your head? They may say you're weak, you're not good enough, or you're an imposter. Or maybe they ask questions. Who do you think you are? Why do you think you can do that? Who do you think you're fooling?

We all have doubts and fears, but sometimes these feelings are based on lies we've told ourselves. They become stumbling blocks because they cause us to hold ourselves back. It doesn't have to be this way.

The next time you feel powerless, question the messages you're telling yourself. Are they truths based on evidence or falsehoods based on feelings? Choose to be strong, ignore the lies, and carry on.

Tied

I ask to be untangled,
To be free.
Yet I stand here, firmly knotted,
With my own fearful hands
Upon the strings.

Capabilities

I will never know
What I am truly capable of
If I never seek to challenge
My perceived capabilities.

When I was writing *Looking Back and Running Forward*, I didn't plan to include poetry other than the poem I wrote for my husband's funeral. However, when I was finishing the final chapter, a poem came to me. "Beautifully Broken" is that poem.

Some people look at their brokenness through a lens of shame or sadness. This poem presents an alternative viewpoint. Everyone is different. Our imperfections and life experiences make us uniquely ourselves. We can embrace our brokenness and be thankful.

Beautifully Broken

Beautifully broken
No place for shame
Most perfectly imperfect
God made me this way

Designed for His purposes
His blueprints unseen
Trusting imperfections
I see not what He sees

In a world of illusions,
A mask I won't wear
Awkwardness unavoidable
The weight I must bear

Beautifully broken
Content in His plan
A Master's creation
Sculpted by loving hands

Before I came to know the Lord, I lived quite selfishly. It was the only way I knew how to live. It wasn't until I began attending church and witnessing the heartfelt words and actions of the people I met there, that I began to wonder if there was another way to live.

Some people say they found the Lord, but the Lord's not lost. We are. The good news is we don't have to wander through this world on our own. There is another way, and it's not hidden. We just need to allow our hearts to be open to it.

Another Way

Oh, how thin the ice we tread upon
When we do not know the solid ground
Lies right beneath our wandering steps
Not hidden away like secrets kept.

What needless suffering we partake
When we only live for our own sake,
And cast aside a much greater worth
For the fleeting treasures on this Earth.

But if only we would stop and look,
The answers are waiting in the Book.
If we'd let them fill our hearts each day,
We'd strengthen to live another way.

What's your idea of a happy place? Maybe it's at home, sitting in your favorite chair and reading a book. Or maybe it's a fun destination where you can enjoy experiences not found at home.

I wrote "Happy Place" when I was longing to get back to a place that I enjoy. It's certainly not my only happy place, but it's the one I was wishing I was at that day.

Everyone needs a break sometimes to escape the burdens of this world and re-energize. Whatever your happy place looks like, enjoy it.

Happy Place

Take me to a happy place
Where yesterday is easily forgotten
And worries of tomorrow cease.
I long to wonder, to play, to laugh
In a place where hours are not counted,
And time is not wasted.
A place where the only moment that matters
Is the moment you're in.
A place of easy smiles and warm hearts.
Take me to a happy place,
If only for a little while.

Why do we spend so much of our day worrying? Fretting about the unknown is a waste of precious time and energy. I know this to be true and yet I still do it far too often.

Sometimes we mask our worry by adopting a pessimistic attitude. We complain about the problems in this world and promote a defeated outlook to those around us.

"Have You Forgotten" is a wake-up call to avoid this mindset. We need only open our eyes to the wonders of nature to be reminded that there is a greater purpose at work. Let that comfort you and dispel the cynicism.

Have You Forgotten

Have you forgotten
The same sun that sets tonight
Will rise again tomorrow?
Look to the birds.
They flutter and glide,
Set on fulfilling their purpose.
They do not fret nor loiter in uncertainty.
Listen to their sweet chatter
And let it fill your soul with hope.
Do not let the darkness deceive you.
Open your eyes to the light.

Have you ever felt like you wanted to try something, but you weren't sure why? Has it ever felt like a little voice inside your head was challenging you to move out of your comfort zone?

This book began with a tiny voice. It began speaking years ago when I was writing poems regularly. It gave me the desire to write a book of poetry. I didn't know if it would ever happen. The yearning faded, but it never completely disappeared.

After I published my memoir, the voice grew stronger. It was then that I accepted the challenge. Even though I was scared to do it, I would publish a book of poetry.

We can sit idly by and ignore the tiny voice that prompts us, or we can bravely dare to do something we've never done before and see where it leads us. The choice is yours.

The Tiny Voice

Submit your mind.
Surrender your ears.
A tiny voice is whispering.
Can you hear it?

It speaks a challenge,
An impossible feat,
Too enormous to consider.
Will you disregard it?

The voice grows stronger,
To the point of distraction,
Nagging you day and night.
Why do you resist it?

Almost screaming now,
The voice persists,
Beckoning you to answer.
What will you do?

Listen to its prompting?
Accept the challenge?
Or, cower back to your comfort?
The choice is yours.

The voice calls to you,
And calls for a reason.
Be brave. Step forward.
Your future is waiting.

A tiny voice makes another appearance in the poem "Share." This poem is an encouragement to bless others by revealing a bit of yourself.

We can't see into other people's hearts. We don't know what they're struggling with by looking at them. They may be dealing with physical or emotional pain. They may be fighting a spiritual battle.

When you share your story, you allow others to make connections. You become relatable. I can learn from your experiences when I understand where you're coming from.

You may never know whether your story helps someone, but that's not the point. The glory isn't for you. All you can do is share.

Share

Someone needs to hear.
>Share.

Though your heart is full of fear,
>Share.

When a tiny voice is speaking,
>Share.

Though they know not what they're seeking,
>Share.

As a vessel unassuming,
>Share.

Of the blessing they're consuming,
>Share.

Trust the author of your story.
>Share.

He will use it for His glory.
>Share.

Motherhood is tough. It's the most important job I've ever had, yet I didn't train for it. The only real training you get with motherhood is on-the-job training. You learn as you go, and you do the best you can.

One thing I've learned is the type of mother I aspire to be is one who earnestly listens when her children speak. Often this means shifting my attention from what I'm doing to focus on them, even when it's inconvenient to do so. I'd rather spend the time listening to whatever my children want to share with me than push them away. These are priceless moments I can't ever get back.

Moments

These are the moments I relish:
When my son shares his latest conquest or discovery,
Going into great detail with his explanation,
All the while, fully knowing
That I don't really understand what he's talking about,
But he tells me anyway
Because it is important to him,
And in his heart, he knows
That if it is important to him,
Then it is important to me.
So, I listen
And ask questions
And embrace these small magical moments
With my son.
They are a blessing.

We go through periods in our lives when we give our all to what we're doing, seizing moments and opportunities with gusto. We have purpose and direction, energized to serve in whatever way we're able.

Then, something changes and we gradually, or sometimes suddenly, stray from the path we were following. Perhaps we just get tired. Or we decide that we're too old or weak. Sometimes we just get lazy.

It's far too easy to fall into the trap of complacency. It's tempting to just sit, put our feet up, and let someone else take over.

Even if you can't physically or emotionally do what you once did, that doesn't mean your to-do list is complete. You can do something, and likely more than you realize. Your journey is not over. Press on.

Butterfly

Does the butterfly give up its flight
Because its wing is torn?
Or does it continue to sip sweet nectar,
A task for which it's born?
If only we could do the same—
Forget the thorns and seek the flowers,
Fulfilling what we're called to do
Until our final hour.

It seems fitting to end this book with "A New Season." Reading a book can be like experiencing a change of seasons. You begin one way, and as you read, your mind wanders and forms new connections. By the end of the book, you're not quite the same as when you started.

We go through seasons in many areas of our lives. We're constantly changing, growing, and transforming into new versions of ourselves. This is a beautiful thing. Let's fully embrace the season we're in and be thankful for the journey that led us here.

A New Season

Cast away your tired leaves,
Yesterday's spring and summer.
Let shine the brilliance of your trunk,
Strong from many winters.
Reach deep your roots into the warmth,
The solid ground that anchors you.
Dance with the wind and rejoice.
A new season has begun.

I hope you enjoyed reading *Poems of Praise and Pain*. You can help others find this book, and show your support for my writing, by leaving a review online where you purchased it. Thank you!

Follow me at:
www.facebook.com/HKinneyWriter
www.instagram.com/HKinneyWriter

Would you like to receive some positive inspiration each month? Subscribe to the free *Updates & Encouragement Newsletter* at www.heidikinney.com.

You may also like:

Looking Back and Running Forward:
Discovering what it means to be broken
ISBN 9781737255703

www.ingramcontent.com/pod-product-compliance
Lightning Source LLC
Chambersburg PA
CBHW021003150626
46549CB00012BA/983